Animals
at Home

FIRST EDITION
Series Editor Deborah Lock; **US Editor** John Searcy; **Art Editor** Mary Sandberg;
Pre-Production Producer Nadine King; **Producer** Sara Hu; **Picture Researcher** Rob Nunn;
DTP Designer Ben Hung; **Jacket Designer** Mary Sandberg; **Reading Consultant** Linda Gambrell, PhD

THIS EDITION
Editorial Management by Oriel Square
Produced for DK by WonderLab Group LLC
Jennifer Emmett, Erica Green, Kate Hale, *Founders*

Editors Grace Hill Smith, Libby Romero, Michaela Weglinski;
Photography Editors Kelley Miller, Annette Kiesow, Nicole DiMella;
Managing Editor Rachel Houghton; **Designers** Project Design Company; **Researcher** Michelle Harris;
Copy Editor Lori Merritt; **Indexer** Connie Binder; **Proofreader** Larry Shea;
Reading Specialist Dr. Jennifer Albro; **Curriculum Specialist** Elaine Larson

Published in the United States by DK Publishing
1745 Broadway, 20th Floor, New York, NY 10019

Copyright © 2023 Dorling Kindersley Limited
DK, a Division of Penguin Random House LLC
22 23 24 25 26 10 9 8 7 6 5 4 3 2 1
001-333458-May/2023

A catalog record for this book
is available from the Library of Congress.
HC ISBN: 978-0-7440-6804-7
PB ISBN: 978-0-7440-6805-4

DK books are available at special discounts when purchased in bulk for sales promotions, premiums,
fundraising, or educational use. For details, contact: DK Publishing Special Markets,
1745 Broadway, 20th Floor, New York, NY 10019
SpecialSales@dk.com

Printed and bound in China

The publisher would like to thank the following for their kind permission to reproduce their images:
a=above; c=center; b=below; l=left; r=right; t=top; b/g=background

Alamy Stock Photo: Avalon.red / Anthony Bannister 16cr, 16bc, David Tipling Photo Library 11cla,
INTERFOTO / Zoology 8cb, mauritius images GmbH / Eckart Pott 7b, Nature Photographers Ltd / Laurie Campbell 27br,
Nature Picture Library / Kim Taylor 21cra; **Dorling Kindersley:** Jerry Young 3, 14cl, 22cr; **Dreamstime.com:** Bigphoto 19,
Chase Dekker 13, Georgy Dzyura 10, Gerra 22b, Haunterofthewoods 13tr, Paul Maguire 7t, Marcin Mierzejewski 26cr,
Ondřej Prosický 9, Ilja Enger Tsizikov 11tr, Vladimirdavydov 2c, Yeti88 30; **Getty Images:** The Image Bank / Andrew Fox 8clb;
naturepl.com: Stephen Dalton 21ca, Yva Momatiuk & John Eastcott 12; **Shutterstock.com:** Neale Cousland 11crb,
Pierre Williot 27ca, Pong Wira 18br

Cover images: *Front:* **Dreamstime.com:** Dannyphoto80; **Getty Images:** Moment Open / Jose A. Bernat Bacete b;
Back: **Dreamstime.com:** Flashvector bl

All other images © Dorling Kindersley
For more information see: www.dkimages.com

For the curious
www.dk.com

Animals
at Home

David Lock

Contents

Home

What is your home like?
Is it cozy and dry?

Animal homes are all shapes
and sizes.
They keep animals and their
babies safe and warm.

hermit crab shell

rabbit warren

stork nest

Making Homes

Bird Nests

Some animals build
their own homes.
Many birds make nests.
Some use mud, twigs, or grass.

weaverbird nest

ovenbird nest

beak

Other birds peck out holes
in trees.
They use their beak to build
their homes.

Burrows and Mounds

Some animals dig burrows under the ground.

Moles dig their tunnels using their sharp front claws.
They push the soil away, making hills above the ground.
They eat the worms and insects that fall into their tunnels.

burrow

mole
hill

claws

Termite Homes

Termites use soil to build
their homes, too.
Thousands of these insects
work together to build a home,
called a mound.

Beaver Lodges

Beavers build their homes by weaving sticks together with their feet.
Their large homes are called lodges.

The beavers get in and out of the lodge through an underwater entrance.

lodge

Shells

Some animals live in shells.
Tortoises and snails can
tuck into their shells.
The shells get bigger
as the animals grow.

shell

Cocoons

Some insects, like silkworms, make their own silk threads.

The larvae weave the silk around themselves to make cocoons. Their homes keep them safe as they change shape, grow wings, and become moths.

silkworm

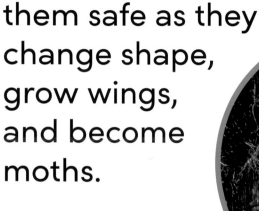

cocoon

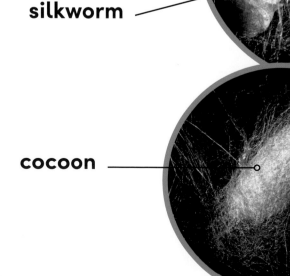

A silk moth outside
its cocoon

Spiderwebs

Spiders can make silk, too. They use it to make their homes.

Some spiders make webs. They eat the insects that get stuck to the strong, sticky silk.

Other spiders build silk-lined burrows with a hidden trapdoor.

trapdoor spider burrow

Beehives and Wasp Nests

Honeybees make beeswax
in their bodies.
They use it to make
their beehive.

honey

There are many six-sided cells inside the hive.

Bees store honey in some cells. The queen lays eggs in other cells.

bee larva

Paper Wasps
Like bees, paper wasps are insects that live in groups. They chew wood into pulp and use it to make their nests.

Finding Homes

Piles of leaves, rotting logs, and compost heaps may not seem like good places to make a home.

beetle

hedgehog

But many small animals
feed and live in these
warm, damp places.

ant

toad

Tide Pools

Sea stars, crabs, and some small fish make their homes in tide pools.

sea star

They live in the water that collects between the rocks on the seashore.
Shellfish and anemones cling to the rocks.

shellfish

anemone

Tree Homes

Trees are homes for many animals.

Birds make nests in the branches.

Squirrels build homes called dreys in the branches, too.

Insects live in the bark or on the leaves.

drey

Badger Burrows
Badgers build burrows called setts among the tree roots. They eat hundreds of earthworms from the soil every night.

Our Houses

We are not the only ones who live in our dry, cozy houses.

Bats may sleep in the attic. Tiny bugs live in the carpets and the furniture.

We all want
a warm
home with
food nearby.

Glossary

Anemone
A small sea animal that attaches to hard surfaces like rocks

Compost
A mixture of rotting plants and vegetables

Drey
A squirrel's home

Larva
A wormlike form that hatches from the eggs of many insects

Sett
A badger's home

Tide pool
Water that collects between the rocks on a seashore

Warren
A rabbit's home

Index

Quiz

Answer the questions to see what you have learned. Check your answers in the key below.

1. What do some birds use to make nests?

2. What kind of home do tortoises and snails live in?

3. How do moles dig their tunnels?

4. How do beavers get in and out of a lodge?

5. What kinds of animals make silk?

1. Mud, twigs, or grass 2. A shell 3. With their sharp front claws
4. Through an underwater entrance 5. Silk moths and spiders